THE MILLS & BOON®
MODERN GIRL'S GUIDE TO

Growing Old
Disgracefully

HQ
An imprint of HarperCollinsPublishers Ltd.
1 London Bridge Street
London SE1 9GF

This hardback edition 2017

1

First published in Great Britain by
HQ, an imprint of HarperCollinsPublishers Ltd. 2017

A catalogue record for this book is
available from the British Library

ISBN: 978-0-00-824481-1

Printed and bound in Italy

Funny, feisty and feminist:
The Mills & Boon Modern Girl's Survival Guides.

.

Introduction

When it comes to ageing, the aches, regrets and indignity of not getting ID'd in Asda when you buy your nightly two-pints-of-gin-and-a-lime are just the beginning. There's also the unexpected crying and the onset of insomnia – then, the existential angst, half-finished projects, and the tedious anecdotes of your equally long-lived companions to contend with.

And let's not forget the bad marriages to unsuitable people who somehow won't kick the bucket, the unfortunate tattoos and the terrible dinner parties. Frankly, the list goes on. But at least you're not dead – and, as my good friend Mae West once remarked, 'You only get to live once, but if you do it right, once is enough.' So, now you're in your dotage, you should use every opportunity to make the most of the time you have left. Let go of your boring, well-behaved self and set your bad side loose. This book – helpfully printed in big, easy-to-read type for your failing old-person eyes – will give you the low-down on drinking, swearing and spending all the cash that your family were hoping to inherit.

And if by the end (which is drawing ever nearer) you're still in any doubt about how to wholeheartedly head over to the dark side, just remember the five magic words: 'WHAT WOULD OLIVER REED DO?'

As ever, Ada

Attention

Since Mel turned 60, she has been experimenting with costumes to see whether anything can make anyone notice her when she walks down the street.

It hasn't worked, but she'll be the one laughing when her pension payments start rolling in.

Bucket List

Jan's Bucket List:

1) Swim with dolphins
2) Learn to play the ukulele
3) Take romantic holiday in Paris with exotic lover
4) Find exotic lover
5) Go on ostrich ride
6) Set realistic life goals

Cleanliness

<u>How My Standards Have Developed As I've Aged:</u>

I'm going to keep this new place spotless!

I probably only need to vacuum once a month

The pink mould on those cups is actually very pretty

The authorities haven't stuck a biohazard sign
on the door so basically everything's fine

I will definitely clean that biohazard
sign sometime next week

Crushes

Rita, Helen and Sue have disguised themselves as a Spode tea set.

They are on their way to Harrogate, in the hope that the fit one off *Antiques Roadshow* will offer them a personal appraisal.

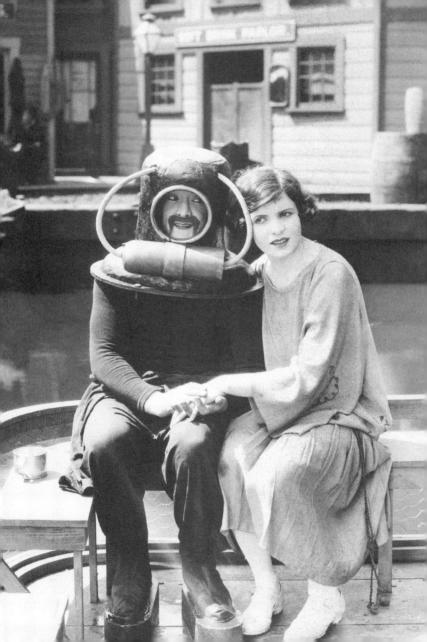

Diminished Expectations

<u>How My Romantic Expectations
Have Developed As I've Aged:</u>

I wonder which member of *Take That* I should pick?

I wonder which bookshop I'll be browsing, coffee shop I'll be sitting in or river bank I'll be strolling along when I meet The One?

I wonder whose wedding I'll be at when I finally get laid (Wayne doesn't count)?

Yeah, whatever, I guess Wayne will do – even with his 'unique' sense of style.

Dinner Parties

Piece of advice #3:

As long as a conversation about mortgages takes place, the room is mainly made up of couples, and something is en croûte, it is officially a Dinner Party.

And at Dinner Parties, you can officially drink as much as you like and still feel sophisticated in the Uber on the way home.

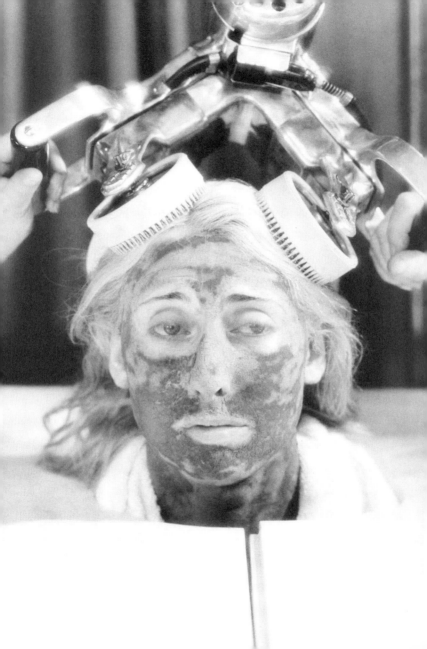

DIY Facelifts

Look Ten Years Younger!

1) Smooth out fine lines and wrinkles with some really tight elastic bands and as much Sellotape as you can attach to your giant jowls!

2) Problem flaky skin – sandpaper and a couple of Jeff's floor polishers will do the job!

3) The dust from the bottom of a Dorritos bag is a great substitute for bronzing powder!

Drinking

Perks of Getting Older #1:

Sure, being twenty-two, getting sh*tfaced and coming home at 3am clutching a donner kebab instead of a handbag was fun.

But, these days, Carol can drink as much as she likes at the races with no danger of ending up in the tabloid press under the headline: 'BOOZY BEAUTIES BRING SHAME ON THE FAIRER SEX'.

She'll drink to that!

Entertaining Yourself

Adele has found that taking out her false teeth and repeating the word 'blancmange' over and over again to those PPI callers has worked wonders for her self-esteem issues.

Failing to Learn

It was the fifth time Rashida had found herself in this exact same situation, and she had to acknowledge that perhaps it was time she made some lifestyle changes.

Fashion

<u>Perks of Getting Older #2:</u>

You don't have to worry about whether the zebra look is currently 'all the rage' or not.

You just have to commit.

Finally Snapping

That feeling when your midlife crisis is more
enjoyable than you imagined it would be.

Gym Bunny

Piece of Wisdom #1:

A single visit to the gym can be mentioned to friends and colleagues for six whole months.

In fact, even joining a gym is enough to provide a healthy glow of smug self-satisfaction for anything up to five weeks.

Hangover

Perks of Getting Older #3:

People always talk about hangovers getting worse
the older you get, but Abi has discovered that
now she is 'a woman of a certain age' she can
make her boss feel awkward by talking about weak
bladder control and use that extra toilet time to
have a nap in a cubicle.

Hobbies

Turns out there is a very fine line between 'taking up a nice, age appropriate hobby like scrapbooking' and 'looking a lot like a sociopath in a crime drama'.

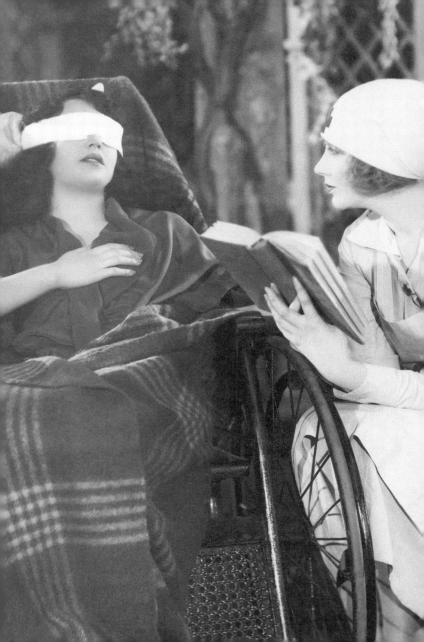

Infirm

Doris has been feeling fine for weeks now,
but she reckons she can squeeze out another six
months of being waited on hand and foot if she
occasionally stops eating her Milk Tray long enough
to say, 'Oh, what I wouldn't give to have my
youthful vigour back!'.

Inspire the Youth

Gwen has told the children about her new hip, her heart stent, her knee replacement and her laser eye surgery.

She is now explaining how she and her cyborg kind will take over their world.

Jealousy

<u>Piece of Wisdom #2:</u>

Manage the anxiety caused by your best friend's seemingly effortless ability to tick off all the important life milestones by replacing them with a nice horse.

Like best friends, horses are extremely loyal companions.

Unlike best friends, there's no danger of them getting married to a reliable man called 'Alan', moving to Surrey or clogging your social media feeds with a billion pictures of their annoying baby.

Kindred Spirits

A shared love of Piña Coladas and walks
in the rain brought them together.

A mutual love of Crown Bowls and Mastermind
kept the love alive.

Now, in the mellow autumn of their lives, Renée and
Ralph are united by a shared hatred of pretty much
everything and everyone on the planet.

Limbering Up

One fun thing about aging is that Liz gets to constantly surprise herself with all the exciting new noises she now unintentionally makes.

Sometimes, it's a sort of groan, like a sad whale.

At others, it's more like a muffled foghorn.

The strenuous activities that cause her to make these noises include 'standing up', 'sitting down' and 'picking up a mug of tea'.

Mastering A Skill

Bella got her black belt in Karate aged fifteen.

At seventeen, she passed her driving
test with one minor.

But, aged thirty-seven, she's just eaten
twenty-three pies in twenty minutes - and
she's literally never been prouder.

Millennials

Ways in Which I Have Tried to Pass
Myself Off as a Millennial:

Mentioning how much I like all the memes

Shouting the word 'emoji'

Wearing an aeroplane hat to show that
I am down with technology

Remembering not to say I'm 'down with'

Failing to get a proper job because of
the tanked economy

Mortality

Ways to Avoid Thinking About Mortality:

Don't ever click on those 'you'll never guess what the baby from the cover of *Nevermind* looks like now!' posts

Don't ever write the date down

Don't hang out next to big creepy clocks and foreboding shadowy hands – this one should be obvious

Nostalgia

When Frieda was nine, she was a Space Invaders addict who spent her days shrieking the theme tune to *Crackerjack* over and over while hyped up on Dib-Dabs.

But if giving her niece a tyre and a stick and telling her she'll never know real fun until she's tried it might get her to switch off that bloody make-your-own-music-video app then she's willing to give it a go.

Outings

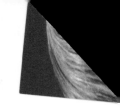

<u>Rebecca and Daphne's celebration of receiving
their joint senior membership of the National
Trust – Itinerary</u>

10.30 a.m. Rearrange all the letter mugs in the gift
shop to spell 'Knobber'

10.50 a.m. Create a 'living history' exhibit from an
ancient suit of armour and some William Morris tea
towels

11.05 a.m. Push a security guy in the ornamental
lake in an attempt to recreate the iconic 'Colin Firth
as Mr Darcy' scene

11.09 a.m. Coach home

Over-sentimental

<u>Things That Set Phyllis Off Now She is Thirty-five:</u>

Random acts of kindness

Remembering they no longer make
Bovril flavour crisps

The 'special piano theme' they
sometimes do on EastEnders

Adverts for donkey sanctuaries

Pretty much any dog GIF

Philosophy

Betty assumed that there would come a point in her life when she would start pondering the big questions - the nature of existence; what happens when you die; destiny versus free will.

But, nope, turns out she's still mostly thinking about Quavers.

Questionable Sexiness

Valerie's impromptu staircase striptease has lost a *little* of its erotic spontaneity due to the three quarters of an hour it's taken her to remove her thirty-five layers of thermals.

Regrettable Tattoos

<u>A List of My Many Regrettable Tattoos:</u>

The 'maggoty skull' I got during
my goth phase

The full back-panel of boy band Westlife
I got during my Westlife phase

The horse I got to cover the Westlife tattoo
which came out looking more like a fat ant

The 'Cleggmania' tattoo (actually, I have
no regrets in this department)

Retirement Issues

One unexpected consequence of suddenly having endless days to fill is watching endless episodes of *Man Versus Food* on afternoon TV.

Now, every meal has become a Big Food Challenge for Daphne and Roxanne.

Even afternoon tea at Claridge's.

Romance

Fun Ways to Keep the Magic Alive:

Leave romantic notes on the fridge saying cute
things like 'Buy some damn milk, why don't you
ever remember to buy the damn milk,
how hard is it really?'

Role-play by calling your partner the name
of the one who got away

Go to a creepy masked swingers party
and instantly regret not being home on the
couch watching *Countryfile*

Second Childhood

It turns out your second childhood is exactly the same as your first childhood, except that this time there's a litre bottle of vodka hidden inside Jemima, your favourite doll.

Slack Parenting

Oh, sure, everyone focuses on the 'you let him get into the elephant enclosure' part, but they all ignore the 'he was reading a book' bit, so frankly I think my laissez-faire approach to parenting isn't as shoddy as people make out.

Technology Fail

First time ever on eBay.
Didn't realise I was bidding.
Accidentally bought a giant pig.
With weirdly human eyes.

Yes - meant I had to move to the country
a little earlier than expected. On the plus side,
she's house-trained, doesn't sweat and the dog
likes her a lot.

Turning Nasty

This? Oh, it's just the skull of the last guy who said *'but when is there going to be an international men's day?'*

Unfinished Projects

In her heart of hearts, Valerie knows that this half-finished painting will end up in her attic along with the first two chapters of her novel, the *Teach Yourself Swedish* book, the violin, and the pet hawk she got back when she decided she would 'get into falconry'.

Man, she should really check on that hawk - they probably need feeding or something.

Very Important Epiphanies

Pieces of Wisdom #4 5 & 6:

4) It is OK to walk out of a boring film

5) It is OK to take yourself out to dinner

6) It is OK to start punching stuff when you realise that people who were literally being born while you were clubbing are now legally old enough to go clubbing themselves

Wisdom

<u>Useless Advice That Jean Enjoys Passing
On to the Next Generation:</u>

1) Paint your silk stockings on using gravy as a
cheap alternative to the black market!

2) Get a student grant rather than a loan because
you don't have to pay the grant back!

3) Buy a flat in 1952 at 1952 prices!

X*** You

A long time ago, Charlotte might have had the levels of patience required to maintain a calm, polite demeanour during a showdown with her bank's customer services.

Those days are gone.

Your Boring Anecdotes

For the ninth time, Veronica has embarked on her story about how she once met Michael Ball when she was shopping in Homebase for something to take the limescale off her taps.

Except it wasn't Michael Ball, only someone who looked like him, but with different hair and a different face.

And it wasn't Homebase, or taps.

But it was definitely limescale.

Zest for Life

Faced with the increasing existential horror of existence Estelle has tried a lot of different coping strategies – mindfulness, positive thinking, affirmations, exercise.

The one she has found to be most effective is 'curling up into a ball and sobbing'.

About Ada Adverse

Ada Adverse hasn't told anyone her correct age since 1982 on principle, but is happy to admit privately to having been in her forties for four decades now. Genetically blessed with youthful skin and short sight, she's sure she has never looked better – and, thanks to a strict regime of mindfulness, eight hours of sleep a night and a double gin with her cornflakes, she's never felt better, either.

About Mills & Boon®

Since 1908, Mills & Boon® have been a girl's best friend.

We've seen a lot change in the years since: enjoying sex as a woman is now not only officially fine but actively encouraged, dry shampoo has revolutionised our lives and, best of all, we've come full circle on gin.

But being a woman still has its challenges. We're under-paid, exhaustingly objectified, and under-represented at top tables. We work for free from 19th November, and our life-choices are scrutinised and forever found lacking. Plus: PMS; unsolicited d*ck pics; the price of tights.

Sometimes, a girl just needs a break.
And, for a century, that's where we've come in.

So, to celebrate one hundred years of wisdom (or at least a lot of fun), we've produced these handy A-Zs: funny, feisty, feminist guides to help the modern girl get through the day.

We can't promise an end to the bullsh*t.
But we can offer some light relief along the way.